Songs Sharp & Tender

Songs Sharp & Tender

Poems by

Carol L. Park

© 2024 Carol L. Park. All rights reserved.
This material may not be reproduced in any form, published,
reprinted, recorded, performed, broadcast,
rewritten, or redistributed without
the explicit permission of Carol L. Park.
All such actions are strictly prohibited by law.

Cover design by Shay Culligan
Cover image is a composite of two original photos by Mitchell Luo
and Alfons Taekema, sourced from Unsplash.
Author photo by Julie Kitzenberger

ISBN: 978-1-63980-617-1

Kelsay Books
502 South 1040 East, A-119
American Fork, Utah 84003
Kelsaybooks.com

To Collin Park, my husband still

Acknowledgments

Many thanks to the editors of the following publications where my poems appeared, some in earlier versions:

Black Fox: "Coupling at Wawona" (previously "The Faithful Couple of Wawona")
Black Poppy Review: "Mother's Proverbs," "Blood Red Bricks"
The Broadkill Review: "That Cat"
California Quarterly: "Evacuating with Smoked Chickens"
The Clay Jar Review: "The Pleasure of Water"
Ekstasis Magazine: "Glimpsing the Better Part"
Foreshadow: "Bark Peeled Back," "Spiraling Songs"
Ginosko Literary Journal: "A Large Room's Sole :: Light," "Monticello Marvels," "Misguided Spring," "Light Touch—the Us" (previously "Sex as We Age"), "Within the In-Laws' House," "Hand Tailored," "Hard on Granny," "Sailing to Strange Harbor," "The Mix"
The Haight Ashbury Literary Journal: "Ax in Glacial Ice" (previously "For My Daughters")
Heart of Flesh: "Being an Us"
The Lindenwood Review: "Lime the Mud"
The Looking Glass Review: "Tending the Fragile," "Out of Alignment"
Minerva Rising: "Caged in Season"
Monterey Poetry Review: "Roses, Song and Apricots"
New Contexts: "Dust Coats the Blossoms" (previously "What My Dear Has Come To"), "Leaves Come Aflame" (previously "Bare Beauty"), "Wasting Time in Greece"
Poemographs for Peace: "Bald Eagle," "Dandelion," "What Grass"
Shark Reef: "Find a Drop of Blood" (previously "What Lingers")
Slant: "The Keeper's Manifesto"
Tiny Wren Lit: "Strange Saint"

Contents

Part I

A Garden Apart	15
Ax in Glacial Ice	16
Cut Out	17
Bark Peeled Back	19
Within the In-Laws' House	20
Sailing to Strange Harbor	22
Under Mother	23
The Keeper's Manifesto	24
Captain Spock	26
Dust Coats the Blossoms	29
Coupling at Wawona	31
Exhale the Alps	32
The Mix	33
Druid	34
Evacuating with Smoked Chicken	35

Part II

Leaves Come Aflame	39
Outside Cardiac Care	41
Caged in Season	42
Chill and Light	43
Roses, Songs and Apricots	44
Kindness to the Rooster	45
Mapless	46
Hand Tailored	48
Floral Mouths	49
Light Touch—the Us	51
Tending the Fragile	52
Dandelion	53
Sticky Window	54

Over My Yard's End	55
Priceless in Home	56
Pleasure of Water	57

Part III

Five A.M. Risers Find the Prize	61
What Is Death?	63
Grecian Ghost	64
Outside My Window	66
Sister Dance	67
Blood Red Bricks	68
Family's Coleman	69
Mother's Proverbs	70
That Warm Drawl	71
That Cat	72
What Grass!	73
Fires Pillow Us	74
Aftermath	75
Lime the Mud	76
California Hills, 4 P.M., Mid-April	77
Island Serenity	79
Revolting Feet	80
Glimpsing the Better Part	81

Part IV

Forgetting in Kauai	85
Strange Saint	87
Out of Alignment—Family Splits	88
Bald Eagle	90
Misguided Spring	91
Find a Drop of Blood	92

Monticello Marvels	94
A Large Room's Sole :: Light	97
After Morning News	99
Nectared Quiet	100
To Nike of Athens	101
Wasting Time in Greece	102
Colors Blend	104
Bursting Out	105
Spiraling Songs	107

Part I

One of the hallmarks of emotional maturity is to recognize the validity of multiple realities and to understand that people think, feel, and react differently. Often we behave as if "closeness" means "sameness."
—Harriet Lerner

A Garden Apart

A parade of flat, black hats & long gowns
drape the graduates—my own among them.
They shout of freedom from grades & tests.
A thousand cameras record their triumph.

After, in a garden nearby, a breeze parts
bleak clouds. Twin dogwoods waltz
while I watch

sweaty hands carry boxes from dorms
& press to chests black-framed diplomas,
facing jobs where bosses pinch female
hips or ignore "girlish" worth with impunity.
A world where friends go distant. Hearts
misperceive or chill through instant messaging.

Their futures look a blooming, but dogwoods'
masses of ovals travel from green & full
to tapered & though their blossoms
of stars abound, winter
shrivels & withers.
Drop.

Congrats, I write.
Heart mixed—
wind gusts
blossoms, leaves,
hearts & minds
a yard, a sun, apart.

Ax in Glacial Ice

Before you knew me,
I pedaled ten miles each way
through fields green until the earth's rim—
all to tutor a farm worker's child.
Through thickening dusk on narrow lanes,
lacking helmet or headlamp, I fought
my way to a clueless dormmate.
On my own after graduation, I grappled
with Greek, housemates, and The Palisades'
huge boulders. Sleeping bag, tent,
and rations weighted my pack. Toe holds
missing, I tottered over head-cracking rocks.

My daughters, I perceive your fear,
your feats, your risks—threading among
throngs of Hanoi motorbikes,
or your ascent—jabbing
crampons and ax into glacial ice.

Do your adventures ready you
for what burgeons today? Fear,
and "Christian" nationalism.
Oh, my children of mixed
race—such dark-haired, tender beauties—
what assaults might it bring you?

My feats recede undivulged.
I slide a smooth granite slope of time
where toe holds prove elusive.

Cut Out

I sprinkle snowflakes of flour
on a plastic sheet.
        The hard ball of dough softens.
I'll roll it flat with my mother's
        faded, weary rolling pin.

In the decade prior, carols merrily sounded.
        What delight for daughters & me
to mix or press the metal shapes: bell, candy
cane, Christmas trees & angels.
The sprinkling of red sugar crystals.

Today I wield the tools for shaping,
        alone. Gone—darling babe
sucking my breast, later slim & stubby
        straw in box of purple juice. Gone:
spills & sticky, needy toddlers' hands,
dodging traffic & racing the clock as I played
driver to lessons of piano or dance.

New freedoms for all—driver's license,
texting, Instagram, teen road trips—
        all thrills welcome.
Today, liberties from well-launched
        kids no longer trill virtuoso.
Knee & shoulder aches alternate.

A mysterious baby grows
        inside my daughter's form.
One day a one-year-old will wobble,
        clasp a wooden spoon & stir—
ablaze to sprinkle green or red sugar.

Push & press, back & forth
     the well-grained, vintage pin
still rolls a buttery, sweet dough—
     ragged edges ever on its circle—

Bark Peeled Back

My friend and I leave our suburbs for a former
freeway—Skyline Boulevard tops a ridge,
overlooking coast and cities. We whiz past
spreading oaks, moss hanging from their limbs.

We talk of close family—how
remote they've turned. A stretch of
firs slopes down. Then clouds of slate
froth, engulf their dusty green.

Fog hides our aches and doubts
churning deep—how to make
of midlife days some lasting art?
What comes at sixty? Parked,

we hike through chilly mist
on paths of needles, and look to
distant peaks—their forms soft today,
their blue like faded Bone China.

"Poison oak—don't let the red leaves
fool you," says my friend. "Yeah,
I learned a decade back. Don't you love
that madrone with its bark peeled far

back?" I pause to snap a photo
of pale underparts, ruddy protection
curling down. How much will I expose
of my drooping heart? Next pale stones

line our path—tiny and precise as
bricks set in symmetry—what expert mason
laid it? I snag a chunk for recalling
momentous hours, unexpected bounty.

Within the In-Laws' House

My husband and I stay a week
      with his parents of Oahu—
their parents from Korea.
        Complexities
            confront.
Eight AM kimchi, rice, and sausage of the Portuguese kind.

Comes a query from my new mom—I reply:
    The pad left my back hurting.
      Shame clouds her coal-dark eyes—
my Anglo manner too transparent.

Should I curtain frank thoughts?
      If I seal my lips,
will I fit in
      and safeguard love?
Customs diverge—how much—
      how can I
curl and smooth my tongue—
      screen my eyes—hide first thoughts?

I'm of the kind
      who jailed this land's queen,
imposed rule, stole lands from natives—grew rich
      on pineapple and cane—on plantation
land my Love's grandma once labored
      in thirst and sweat for paltry wages.

We escape to the beach—
        foaming water surges to the sea—so clear
I glimpse dark gaps between big rocks
        appearing perilous—obsidian keen?—
yet gorgeous in their turmeric, rust,

        and volcanic black—yet if a foot's
placed wrong, a tumble would gash my knee,
        or I'd wrestle a heel that's stuck.
My beloved crosses the rushing river with his sister.
        Am I forgotten—
                abandoned? I hesitate.
My jaw clenches, yet he returns.
        His smile emboldens
                for my crossing.

Sailing to Strange Harbor

Did panic grip as you leaned past the large boat's rail—bye-bye to family and all in Busan? So long ago—no phones, rare mail.

Did you mutter in Korean during Angel Island's immigrant processing? Cringe when meeting your fiancé? First glance told you what a lying photo you held—this man thirty years older.

Lying on your pad on the shanty floor of a plantation, perhaps you bit your salt-sore lips. Stifled tears. That first night, what thoughts after his groping? The spontaneous stiffening and recoiling.

He had the right to what he paid for. Perhaps you knew little of that which goes inside—did your tender drops of blood terrify?

When he died months later, did you blame yourself? Perhaps relief at his demise dampened the fear of the storm in your eyes.

Korean sisters found a man to wed you, father children, earn the wages. While he labored, you worked as able—babes at play or sheltered near you.

How long till he despaired at harsh work, scant earnings? Did you seize his money before it went to drink? Perhaps you prayed. How mistaken your father: *no cruelty to converts in that new land.*

Later in a canning plant, acid ate your hands—still your savings bought a home. You never met your kin again. Yet you survived the voyage, mastered strokes, and though the decades swam so strong.

Inspired by my grandmother through marriage, and the book written about her by her deceased daughter Bessie Park. Myung Okie arrived as a picture bride to Honolulu at age 19, 1917.

Under Mother

I dip bare toes in murky water.
Wide hips of Mommy fit close beside me.
Thick yarns of moss choke the creek.
Water bugs like petticoats skate on top.

Mommy sits on dirt beside me, our arms
& feet sweat from summer heat.
Water bugs like parasols top our tiny pond.
Dark & light do dapple hidden spots.

Calves & feet cool from baking sun.
Oak & shrub enclose us in a room.
Dark & light dapple hidden hearts.
Boulder, pond & room—my sweet shelters.

Thick shrubs & oak limbs hide true forms—
Mom's sweet at church. At home, the accusations.
My room, pond or granite make good crying spots.
Don't talk to your sisters about me, she sternly warns.

Wear finery for church. At home, ugly words & tone.
Siblings leave. I'm the foci for her anxious thoughts.
Don't tell my faults, she insists. No secrets to my friends.
I date. She castigates, *You're the world's most selfish.*

I move out. She leaves messages, *where are you?*
Become a mother, I doubt myself. *Am I being selfish?
How can I embody love? Dare I say no?* Weary & wan,
I wiggle in a mucky pond, not knowing what's love,

what's not—I'm chasing
off the skating bugs.

The Keeper's Manifesto

When I took the marriage pledge, I understood little
      of how the residence of engineers and bachelors
spawned an endless list: scrub mold
      from shower tiles and grime from pantry,
sort through a room's worth of lamps and dishes—
what roommates left behind—then visit Goodwill—
      toss the unwanted.

How wash piles up. For years I sorted your clean socks and undies
      after the dryer buzzes. Yours come out moist, not mine.
Men's garments take clothespins on a line.

Over the years I embrace a better approach—
      hang your own, please, and wipe away
your hairs—lines of black on bath and flooring.

I admit—
      my childishness bobs on up:
I gnaw on offenses far too long.

Yet, like the unexpected breeze flapping
heart-shaped leaves of our apricot tree,
      grace gusts in and transports my gaze,

helps recall the curve of your lips, your whipping
eggs for Saturday's griddle, and ear attuned to my
      long stories when you wish for sleep.

Because of you, I make rice, sauté chard and steak—
      they nourish us both. And who am I
to label a man's tee—faded with holes—offensive.

My silly heart.
        I garden, too—lop off disease and suckers,
Let the hose run long and slow beneath our lovely tree.

Voilà—summer brings abundance of luscious, juicy
apricots. My watery choice turns clear—
        good fortune in calling you *Dear.*

Captain Spock

α

I've pledged to screw the lids on tight, but when you grasp
the relish jar from the top, the jar falls from the lid,
glass shatters, and pickle chunks slime—filling
channels of the grout. Vinegar fumes
     your acrid face.

I want to change. You warn me to push tight the fridge's
double doors so their edges meet.
     But my resolves don't stick,
         nor my Post-its to our fridge.
You find its doors ajar one morning. Your tune turns
     sour as the milk. We each choose
         such different parts to sing.

When my soprano trills high, you snap
     back, *Nebulous—mere speculation—*
         how can you say, "You love
         our daughters more than me?"
Your defense does nothing for my tears.

You conceive the corporeal—not the minute dip
of eyebrows or downward tug of lips—pointers
     to galaxies of meaning. What you gave
me shattered and slid so afar.
Can we retrieve our tender speech—
     divulging needs and guilt?
         Affection of
palm on thigh, tenderness in our fingers?

β

"Logic" is your motto and Spock has been your idol
from boyhood. Math and fix-it-projects
     obsess you—Today it's coding.
For your leisure you choose biking, cryptograms,
     your blog, and devour *The Atlantic.*
You rewire our kitchen, yet our hearts
     don't spark.

I took off solo to escape sterile home,
       fit poles together to raise my own
    snug tent and light a Coleman stove. My
salty drops moisten pinto beans on rice. In dusk
     my desired trail disappears—dappled
     light and spongy silence of dirt,
ferns, and redwood bark. Yet come dawn,
       green and burgundy speak Love to me—
some kind Divine—
     easing twisting of my gut. Lullabies return.
At home—we sing tenderly—my hand to yours.

We see a counselor and in her office shelter
     I risk the weeping—the first you see
       my pain.
Her questions a laser
     to my ears—they alert me

to my unconscious deformity.
    Behind my hurt, envy
        behind my rage, fear.
How my need to be the prima donna,
    sent you running to a silent spot.

I learn to say,
    We, not You, to hear
the panic in your voice—what
      I once passed over. To appreciate
        your tenor.
Lips loosen. I add melody to
    your harmony and allow
        your golden arms around me.

Dust Coats the Blossoms

What do you say when your husband lies so
still on the firemen's stretcher?
They heft him out our front door—
screen cinched open.
"See you later?"—our usual words don't fit.

Near emergency's elevated bed—I stand
above him. How is it that only now
do I see the bare circle of his scalp
expanding? The screen's glowing zigzags
show my love's endangered heart—
I shudder at what the nurse jabs
into his skin—what slim threads
keep his heartbeat going.

What do I say moments after
the doctor slips on out—*used to be
M.Ds were older.* Now bucket lists can't
be considered—it's time we ponder
how our bodies shrivel despite
daily berries, stretches—both fun and tedious
health routines. Going forward, will treadmill tests,
heart checks, and various scans steal our hours?

Will you turn prickly sour as my dad?
He lumbers into mind—
hacking, spitting, fuming at his limits—
that blossoming apricot he can longer tend.

You, my love, take pride
in Costco runs or servicing our stove.
Will backaches and sore ribs tarnish
your gentle ways—turn them strict and harsh?

I tremble as I stand by your high bed—
both of us a bare hum—
       unknowns among machines.

Coupling at Wawona

That mammoth redwood trunk awes me—
    what was once twin saplings
leaning on each other. Their roots run shallow—
    vulnerable to toppling—yet

interlaced like fingers—two tender trees
    survived through gales uprooting
others near them.
    Their girth broadened and these two

coarse, cinnamon trunks—press a finger—
    feel how spongy—
        joined as one with blue-
green needles curving around.

I crane my head at this peculiar tree
    spiking skyward. Up and up till
merged trunks split
            some twenty feet up—

dual towers
    from a single base. Partners—we
too—our roots for decades interlocked—
    discover each needs more than

fusion—each requires accepting
    differences in the other. Single below—
double pillars above. We thrust for the celestial—

Exhale the Alps

Isaac rides in a baby pack on his Daddy's shoulders. We four hike on level soil, then up past snowy patches—all new, so green. My heart rockets while the air turns slight, and lungs constrict. My grandson shrieks—do his lungs pang him? Has the asthma gene passed to him? The nearby creek sniggers. A fall from his parents' bed colored his forehead purple. Strong light pinkens his cheeks. I trust in sunscreen—newbie parents on first high-trek with babe slather on none.

We labor up and stop. Far off alps of ghostly blue with glacier striped peaks. I breathe out tension on sponge of fallen needles. A vulture circles. The sleeping babe wakes with lusty yells. Set free, he goes racing recklessly. A large root trips him—oh, the wails! Oh, to have stopped this fall—I'm not in charge. Still—still myself. Drop my pack. Sip the blue. Inhale, exhale alps.

The Mix

Oil and vinegar shine in the shallow bowl—a tasty concoction transforms bread many days old. The chunk of porous whiteness I dip brings up mere grease—olive oil and balsamic separate—blandly coexist—savory combo gone.

Sunshine dandelions turn to fairies—child me loves to blow them free—waltzing with the wind. Pernicious weeds—what passionate, traditional gardeners despise.

Grandchildren reach my waist—yet cry at a mask become soggy—2020 precautions. Wails so shrill I strap hands to my ears. My homemade zucchini bread rejected—my frown a blood red crescent moon. Yet they wiggle within my breasts and burgeon inside—my old heart inflates like some cheery pink bunny won as a carnival prize. They leave but stay unseen. Perhaps a surgeon's tools can extract their darling smiles and my want. Mixed and changed from independence.

Druid

Squirrel's tail twitches
to balance on wizened vine,
scampers up, in, gone.

Evacuating with Smoked Chicken

California's August 2020 lightning storm ignited 600 fires, forcing many to evacuate.

Escaping flames raging close, the chickens
travel hot and panting, crammed within
a huge but flimsy crate—evacuees from
coastal fires. Often braking her sedan,
Chicken Mama braves the winding pass
to bring a varied brood to refuge.

A dozen chickens mutter and moan in front
while two young kids sit in back,
beside two bunnies—all ignorant
of homes incinerated or trees ignited
without warning. A dusty smell and
clucking chorus distract the children.

Hens stand on fellow-poultry backs—
a dozen pressed and mashed, buckling to
centrifugal force of the scores of curves.
An hour drive—their cravings grow
for water, air, and space to fly or wiggle.
Meringue the pullet will suffer no more.

Her beak rams out, then her red neck
through unsealed cardboard flaps.
Glassy eyes rebuke her Mama. Meringue
makes a break—flaps up and out—free
at last—she rises. Mama shrieks—a vision
of feathers blocking vision of the highway,

escaping flames, but a not-so-hot
way of dying. With one hand
Mama crams the squawking rebel
back within her stopgap pen. Uproar
in the rear—laughter of the innocents.

Part II

To be a human among people and to remain one forever, no matter what the circumstances, not to grow despondent and not to lose heart—that's what life is about, that's its task.
—Fyodor Dostoevsky

Leaves Come Aflame

Through my windshield a bramble—denuded
      tree—outside my station wagon
          compels my eyes—naked limbs
months past emerald—frost drips from twining twigs.
Inside the hall my daughter kicks
      an Irish jig—I mingle a locust's woody
          tangles with my mother's mind and
manner—her supple cells dropped, crumbled, dust—
    Alzheimer's a wintering.

Your mother's sweet—my friend's remark—
      I secreted my jumbled shock—could not
lay bare the anger at her barbs and judgments—
      once to her long-unseen niece—*Why is
your tummy a watermelon?*—more—
      to collegiate me—*how dare you wear those
sweatpants out? What will neighbors think
    of me?*
          No retort—silent as I'd been taught.

Yesterday I left her rose-lined senior complex—
      she waved a freckled hand and forearm. So forlorn
          her voice—When will you return?—
her thanks forgotten. Me?
    Content to visit, good
          to go—we're such mixed souls.

Careless cars buzzed the highway—trucks rumbled
      broccoli onward—feedlot stink—lungs
          squeezed—stretched hours—jetting
hazards—home—eager husband—sparkling girls and
          enthused dalmatian.

Today alfalfa fragments—carbon—exhaustion
    pock the glass—
        my frost touched heart—

Outside Cardiac Care

Bullets of rain assault the bricks outside.
Sea green walls swirl around us women
        aching to know our dear ones' fates.
The woman called behind the double doors
rejoins us—terror blazes from orbits of her eyes.

Seated near, a brunette bends low to search her bag.
She bobs up—two fingers hold a smoke.
A wrinkled woman deftly twines two needles.
Their shining rise and fall knits a scarf to wrap
around her husband's neck—a purchase
        of more time.

My weary mother lays shut
behind strong doors, awaiting her exam.
She asked on our drive here, brows crunched,
        Is doing this worth the trouble?
        Sometime, I have to go.

I didn't answer. Her unsaid question,
        Am I worth your bother?
I held her puffy fingers,
        kissed her chalk-dust scalp.

Caged in Season

My cleaning finished, I pause before
Mother's photo—walnut framed—
a cage like her new room. No more camping
days. Gone the thrill of pointing out to me
madrone, poison oak and constellations—
Orion, the Hunter—like Yaeger.

Her home of fifty years lies emptied.
She walks a hall of doors—posted
names of strangers she can't memorize.
No more baking cookies, or misting
camelias. It's Reader's Digest, TV,
and graying silence.

If she ventures on her new grounds,
she'll pluck purple leaves, or snip
a "Peace" bloom and gift a friend
a coral rose. Maybe win a smile, but little
admiration. Is it too much to hope she'll
reenter redwood grandeur of Big Basin
or Tahoe's variegated blues?

Chill and Light

Mother's lids stayed shut, lips unmoving,
chin angled up. Her Adam's apple marked
slowing swallows. Does she care?
The only motion of her body worn
so thin, pricked and threaded with cords
and tubes for monitors and meds.

Her hand freckled from gardening,
once tan, now paled and calloused,
softened—I lift it to my lips.

I'm nearly out the double doors to the night,
when the nurse runs and calls, *Come!*
She's almost gone. Upstairs,
yellow digits spike up
then down, down. Stop.

A death later, I pluck tissues in my car.
On the highway, curves of hills and chill
expands, then the shutting down of light.
Wet wads—my dirtied snow drifts on charcoal mats.
Two hours of deep knowing—she no
longer breathes who heard my reports
of good and rocked no current of envy.

Home, a cut-glass lamp from Mother
beams on my pillow its rose light. Soon,
an unlit hole pulls me under.

Roses, Songs and Apricots

In Mother's old hymn book, pink leaves—once
crimson—picked through forty years of ambles,
flake brittle at my touch.

My small hand within her larger hand. Together
we collected colors at our feet. Her cursive adorns

her hymnal's brown-edged pages—*Play for me*—
still spread open on my shiny piano. I caress
the notes—the way I gave us once both pleasure.

Her small ceramic pot still carries water out to pots.
Its pink daisies sing my childhood uncertainty:
"She loves me, she loves me not."

I wipe clean bird-pecked, half-rotted apricots
in a kitchen bucket, recall the tedium of fulfilling
Mother's many orders, my slaving at her sink.

Once I couldn't stand her Baptist hymnody,
her red roses or homemade jam—so clumpy.
Yet these days I fill jars with tender apricots

and feed a multitude of "Peace" rose roots.
Still, she doesn't leave. Her watering pot
shatters in my grip. I gather its sweet shards.

Twelve months since cremation, still
grief returns in pinkening leaves,
and ragged songbook edges.

Kindness to the Rooster

Jen can't forget how her hands nuzzled down
of her fresh-hatched chicks. Later she rues
how—though deemed the egg-laying
sex—one grows bigger, one turns rooster.

Let no one forget his full tail's
iridescence—that green sheen
curving of Maui who seized the role
of lord over the backyard flock.

Let not Jen's ears forget what made her
run in terror to young ones at 2 AM,
to find them peacefully asleep—not
screaming like a cockerel's yodels.

Let her not forget his never missed
morning summons and twice nightly
disturbances—recall again what
friends said, *you got to get rid of him.*

Let not the children forget the often
repeated squawks of terrified Maple
when Maui chased the little hen. Or
his persistent pecking while she hid.

Let not Jen forget how Maui pulled
her feathers out till Maple came from hiding.
He wrapped his wings around her tight
and perpetuated sexual assault.

Let his owner's mercy be praised—though
Jen wants to wring his neck, tender memories
of his peeps and down prevent her. A friend takes
him on and Maui yields to an older rooster.

Mapless

Maps for parks—contour lines of baby blue
        for canyons & peaks—stuff my pockets
—guides like scriptures I used to pour over,
like teachers citing Greek who lit my way before.
        In these times they've turned to tule fog.

Pyramids of pebbles mark an obscure trail.
Ignorant of my end, I long for mist to lift.
        Still I plod on. Stiff boots burn
throbbing blisters. Clammy socks must go—
        sharp stones puncture soles
while craters of bewildering ache tail.

My marathon fatigues, but I can't pause—
        hunger gnaws. Above, the keen beak
of a circling hawk. A strange cave appears—
I enter, sleep, and—come dawn—emerge to
        firs' pine scent—refreshed and ready.

My tender feet on spiny needles—even they
        pierce. Yet, folds of trillium's
rich leaves bend—so must I. Their tri-
        petalled pink blooms fold as to pray.
I stoop, listen, petition peaks uncharted.

I climb though glacial frosting rumbles—
footholds few. My boot jams into ice—a stiff
        but welcoming group I join.
Clerical collars quote poetry, give out wine, and
        carve a strange yet enticing course.

I toss ambition to the back. Serene again,
        I'm eager for uncharted mountains—
fleeing judgment and certitude in rightness.
        Shame takes the back seat and soft fingers
clasp new hands in women's jail and cedar chapel.

Summitted—a song of joy—I sign so (my name)
        on a log's frayed page among weathered scrawls—
climbers through the ages. They prod me on—
        no staying here. New alps call.

Hand Tailored

But intentions browned & crinkled
like apricot-hearted leaves in autumn.
   A decade from the purchase, I brave again
the project: you in shirt, arms T-framed,
     shoulder seams sagging far beyond.
Clothes make the man—so I think.

   I meant to fit it to you—pierced
fabric with care, intending not to prick
    your soft skin.
I started & stopped the sewing—fearing
  my failure.

Long ago I spied it in a Honolulu shop—synthetic,
not an island-made design of cotton.
    Your lips pressed tight—a signal
  I ignored. You've long disdained such spending.
     Decades-old jeans & tees are fine—to you
—but to me: tattered, faded.

In pandemic isolation, palms quivering, I face the
   needed—irreparable cuts to size shoulder
caps narrow, pierce fabric with gathering stitches.
  I spin a slim thread between moist fingers,
target the needle—a lemon seed of a hole.
   Oh that, it didn't tire me so
  fitting this shirt to you. Still, I benefit
in vision clearing—careless presumptions shifted.

You don't wear it—though completed—
  your choice—
    Honolulu shirts your sister creates.
And more & more I find they're the ones
    befitting: Oahu turtles swimming
a mellow, blue Pacific—

Floral Mouths

Ungentle gusts shake our yard's canopy, once white
        as my wedding gown, but faded now, sullied,
                with flecks like oatmeal dust.
Your desires, my lover, are often as vague
        as your hand on my hip. What and when do
you want? Your aspirations vary: you would-be hero—
        mentor for the needy. You rush on off—
        you flip   an inner switch.

Outside, I sit in rain patter. Wet curtains fuzz
        a pair of wings
                coming straight at me. A hummer's chin
displays red iridescence—a wild flash—quite near,
        his black bead of an eye takes me in,
                intimate scrutiny—he suspends so long
before he zooms to dip forked tongue inside
        our bounteous garden's floral mouths tiny as his beak.

Lover, you peered at me microseconds before your speedy
        mind whizzed on—emails, scheduling appointments,
                on-line reading, and conceiving a mini essay
on grounding, connection, love—
        ours put aside.

You blur flight from imagining lovemaking
        to screen staring—such a hummer you—
so when I place a hand on your back—an invitation
        to pleasure—it's brushed off.
Do I do so to you? A true question.

Please, won't you hover? Expose that tiny crimson
        spot tucked under—whisper out your vulnerable heart.
Perhaps
                even share the gathering of our garden's bounty?
Don't be a bellicose hummer, chasing away
        another, refusing to share with your own kind.
Let's pause together over little
        purple mouths—stems protruding
        from shrubs we've watered. Insert our
        tongues among the little red and white hearts—they
beckon us—lips—
        blooms ready
                for our bodies' pleasures.

Light Touch—the Us

Once you were the one distracted, unmoored—
      today it's me with ambitious ends. I edge away
           from your hand on my hip.

Still, I can't say no to the pillow,
      but you intuit my drift to resolves still undone.

"You're not all here—analyzing the 'hero's journey?'"
      "Yes" I admit. Worries also gust me—
      a catamaran a drifting—rudder broken.

Like a virgin once more
      I dare to unscrew
           my tightened soul.

Let's meld minds today that distraction
      won't gust us far apart.
That sweet rice cake won't settle heavy,
      panging our guts.

Sands in our shining hourglass
      dribble ever faster, taunting us—
           a threat to our merging.

Let's choose to stop proving ourselves.
      I write fewer lines—
           you bike fewer hills.

I remind you again,
      sex starts well before the sheets—
           light touch—unexpected
on my arm. Pleasant pressure—not a pinch—
      on my cheeks still soft and round.

Tending the Fragile

Tears stream from my cherished
teen—stretched out on flowered
couch—she wants no words or touch—
a boyfriend loss. I tip-toe out.

After early warmth, cold droplets
softly bend our daffodil fronds—hollow
stems can't keep high our garden's
sunshine cups. Topple. Grounded.

Mollusks ooze out, forging
slimy trails. Their thin tongues
dressed in savage teeth
rip the trumpeters of spring.

Not so hard to toss the knaves,
tie pliant stems aloft to stakes—fragile
crowns of gold made safe. Oh, for know-
how with the tender bloom of home.

Dandelion

Little fairy seeds
from globe-like mother
blow off—gone the close.

Sticky Window

A double hung window—
>   wooden frame and sill,
>   crevices thick with dirt.

Two hands inside grip and pull.
>   It sticks.
She yanks
>   and slams it shut.

I teeter on an old wooden ladder,
>   wobble near a hedge of roses.
>   A thorn jabs my side.
>   Furious black bees buzz nearby.

I peer between smears on glass. Where stands
>   the sweet babe I tucked within my pink sling?
Nearing three, her soft, fuzzy voice went on nonstop.
>   I soaked it in—faint owies, Disney shows
and Band-Aids. Pocketing her found acorns.

Three decades pass.
>   I hear, "Toss the sling! I run. I'm off."
She changes her name—"Susan" to "Dawn."
Pulls down the light-blocking shade.
>   Of course. It's time.

I climb down, leave off
>   her room's window.
Grounded, my arms still ache to bear her.
At night my ears strain
>   and hear her plaintive voice.

Over My Yard's End

Orange & black checkered
butterfly flits, lifts high
      —foraging, then gardenia-scented flight
over redwood planks of my yard's end.

My own daughter too bursts from
      her seclusion—her transfiguration
jolts a child aroused deep inside—leaving me

to scrabble over yard-high,
      black-and-white peppered boulders—
bearing fingers on rough rock and scraping shins
      to keep from plunging
      over a cliff—yet

I lift my eyes in awe—
paper-thin wings of ripe orange—ecstatic rise
      for her—levitation for me—only a little.

I glance away—what microsecond—
      vanished.

Priceless in Home

Yes, this Mama wants you sheltered
        from fiery fingers.   Ours or
yours.   Our new composite
        roof with fiberglass mat

resists high winds and bounding fire. Note
        we've laid asphalt and mineral tiles,
tossed out touchy wooden or antiquated
        shingles—norms we laid

in youth and taught others—you
        included. Please believe
we're breaking away
        from stodgy thinking—scraping off

devout and stalwart doctrines—what was
        sometimes damning.
        Perhaps they hovered as a hammer poised
to strike aluminum—you a malleable child

Please know Momma wants—aches for
        you—her treasure—near.
            Our love
        transcends   all   difference.

Pleasure of Water

Easter

A head of little emerald leaves
calls from my veggie plot.
        Supple & without blemish—
my beloved lettuce—though in
        my sink—turned end up—
reveals itself as toughened, yellowed
        shriveled stuff.
I dunk the sullied mass in a watery basin
        & rip blighted matter off. Still
leaves remain stuck together, congested
        —dirt hidden.

The blade I grasp is short—yet not too dull
to cut the core that holds a throng of greens,
        glistening, tiny & close.
I pull a clove-like stem off—yet still
        the white solid grasps more.

Upon shaking a bunch, a bug crawls out—
        I cringe at orange & browned ringed abdomen—
long forelegs built for pinching—I fear its bite—
called "earwigs" because once our ears were thought
        the home for such.

Back to cool water's pleasure—
        my fingers opening green ridges—
loosing soil. I dunk & dunk again—
        oh, the many flecks floating, dotting clear water.
Perfection rides high beyond our fingers—
perpetually insisting on one more dunking.
        Enough—grace!

>   Greens make salad—despite
> browned or bitten edges. We'll enjoy them
>   all—lack of flaws not required
> as we the marred yet still friends—
>   gather around our feasting table.

Part III

At some point in life the world's beauty becomes enough.
—Toni Morrison

Five A.M. Risers Find the Prize

June 24, 2022

The warmth swaddles me—moist as an oven
        baking custard—Greece before dawn!
We pilgrims aim towards a remarkable sky—
        scurry on slim lanes—trudge a bridge—
ascend long stairs—wind our way to Chora
        —scarcely learned Greek—"city on a peak."

Unknown route—I scrutinize landing of my feet—
        unsquared stones make for easy stumbles—
surfaces uneven. Rocks extracted—each enormous.
        Were they mortared a thousand years past?
Did slaves hew them? Or did workers heave mallets,
        rupture backs, sweat profusely in summer heat
for paltry sums? I profit from their labor.

Overhead stars proudly beam, but swathes of concrete
claim my eyes—pale and slippery as what birds drop.
Fog eclipses my sight. So little known of my path's
        ending, while I want much, and no rail to abate
a fall. A Humpty Dumpty if I glance too long.

Up and up, I trudge. Our atmosphere thins and cools.
        My asthma-blighted lungs gulp for air—
Below bright dots startle—the drowsy town, Livadi,
        mumbles, *why aren't you sleeping?* and
the pigeons we rouse from roosted slumber echo.

Why do we abandon beds, bust thighs and knees
        to beat the sun's rising? We ache for stellar
phenomena—Jupiter, Mars, Venus, Mercury, and Saturn
        all in a line—we want to be stunned—record it all—
a contest with the dawn.

Black sky fades to navy and we still puzzle past
        stores and homes—up flights & flights of stairs
to a platform for gaping—
        a blue-domed church's patio. We sigh
for Mercury hid behind a cloud, yet

click, click—a bevy of photos
        snatched as planets too swiftly dim in sunlight.
I teeter and whisper, *It's not enough.*
        Where's the light that shatters? Can a mallet
smash steppingstones from boulders of my mind?

What Is Death?

Spring 2020

First, a cough, then fever, fatigue. I stop its
spread by separating from dear family. Resting
in daybed, quite alone, I gasp for breath.

Hooves stomp so hard on my chest, air
won't enter my Covid-prey lungs,
despite all my gulping and heaving.

My wife pretends calm to ward off our children's tears.
To me, "Go see an MD! Far too shallow—your breathing."
Air scarcely enters—despite my chest's heaving.

The news informs of EMT lines at hospitals. Gurneys
jammed up outside. My dear probes for where the odds are best
and drives me there—sharing air—will that advance her death?

Hospital staff triage—swarms of despairing, potential patients.
"We have three young children!" my devoted love protests.
Still air won't enter my lungs, despite my frantic heaving.

In the tent outside, she pleads, "Sedation, please! He needs
intubation." Done! Survived, but memory has vanished—
the best of life has fled—who is it that holds me?—this is
death? No recall of sweetest hours—only anguished trying.

Grecian Ghost

Serifos, Greece

Ancient lettering & strange speech
of townspeople bewilder me—first time
      without my Greek-parsing wife
who once vacationed by my side.

Life goes on in chests of workmen balancing
      on ladders, painting on a moon-like glow,
by window shutters brighter than blue cornflowers—
what she adored. I hope this unspoiled island &
      exultant light will lighten my desert heart.

No kitchen appliances still, I grumble at Reception,
but her dear spirit visits—handwashes cereal bowls &
      smiles—mysterious & faint—melting my cold.
I gently touch her bare, browned shoulder.
      Do you mind this chore?
      No—for me, it's therapy.

The ferry and dirt lane brought me
      to slaps of sea far from the bustle
of Athens's port—
      yet turmoil spoils my mind.
Come afternoon Cyclades gusts—
      whip me, push me,
tousle my mop wild to match my heart.

There's many a pretty girl, but I don't
        look when wind flies a skirt—
it's not hers. I dine early—what she wanted
& I resisted. These black suited waiters wear
        too much cheer for my ragged sea within—

yet I tip them largely
        as my beloved whispers.
I gaze afar—deep azure, serene her voice—
        but ferry's blasts disrupt all
        reverie—too soon I depart her ghost
in this still isle, where solemn sea slaps
        so sweet her whisper.

Outside My Window

Sparrows, finches, jays
snatch seeds from a plastic feeder—
hungrily chase each other.

Sister Dance

We share a room. I look up to sis—she in tight
        bodice, small waist, gauzy skirt—her means
        a boutique job in after-school hours.
She slams the bathroom door. She in, me out of her
        dance and cranberry lips for drive-in kisses.

Paperback pages of Frodo's trek distract. I guide the
        keen needle of Mom's old black Singer
through cotton weave, seam and hem a plain, brown shift—
I spectate while the cool kids jive—first middle school
        dance—no sister-coach in how to do it.

She weds early. I wish to be more than candle girl.
She chooses yellow satin for me. My needle slips—
blood drips. Dingy hall. I pale in the fabric she picked.
        For us Baptists, candy hearts and cake—forget
champagne or dance. No comfort for my restless legs.

Older sister gone from home. She takes accounting, sells
        fancy floral couches—posh we'd seldom sat on.
Her husband flattens nails beside his dad. She confides
some scraps about rooming with her husband's folks.
        His mother knows how to clean house—not
        like ours. His nonna serves four courses.
She gives a hand to dance, sometimes. Then retreats.

Seated on vinyl in sister's boxy Chevy years later,
she pitches to me a type of prayer she's adopted—"tongues."
        Do it—then you'll be a real Christian.
I clasp her booklet and exit. Her dictums crash in metal bin—a
calming clang. Sitting on a rug of yarns I wove myself,
        I complain, "God, aren't my simple words enough?"

Blood Red Bricks

We see things not as they are but as we are.
—Anais Nin

A wall mortared tight, barring
      any sense of self or agency.

A deep well of water—once
      a sisterhood now toxins

turn it poisonous. Or call it
      wounds from a common mother,

still crying out for salve and bandage.
      That small tin box painted with

a red cross we would both finger as if
      rattling Band-Aids were sufficient

remedy. God, stitch up these jagged
      cuts in us both, and between us.

Is there a jackhammer powerful enough
      to fracture my strange sense of you

and you of me? Bloody red, impenetrable
      bricks preclude our peace.

Family's Coleman

Two-burner camping stove
firmed our pancakes, made oatmeal—
disowned, thrown, tossed off.

Mother's Proverbs

Blood is thicker than water. Sticks and stones . . .

Billows surge—higher than our old home—and pummel still
taller rocks. Big sister, a single text in two years between us—

I stopped the words to hush the sister angst—so it seemed.
Christmas comes and the chasm taunts again. Farther down

the shore a tide pool stillness suspends my circling thoughts. Wait.
Then steely sprays of high tide wreck the silence—you, sister

reappear. I long—I think, my fault—if only I . . . but dark relics
hide in a whitecapped sister sea. Despite what our mother said,

blood doesn't stick—no cement. Typhoon words don't vanish.
I ask for a bridge over raging sound. Hyades—nymph sisters—

don't answer but transport—a graceful doe kisses her fawns.
Saplings circle a succoring tree. No need for sisterly voice. I'll be

Queen Anne's lace with tender face held high within a marsh.
I hike smooth paths through towering bushes of berries—sisters

on each side—stems so needled. I pick fruit both sweet and tart—
nourishment—recall us sisters reddening fingers on thorns,
plucking berries under Mother's eyes squeezed so tight.

That Warm Drawl

The near Southern drawl
of my cousin sounds no longer.
Goodbye stifled bird,

following husband's
red fealty—she ignores calls,
texts, sweet chirps of primal bonds.

That Cat

I scribble lines in my mind—that
      feline invades my backyard—
how the white & turd-brown thing
      deposits within among my vegie plot.
How its paws cover
      up & suffocate my baby
chard sprouts. How that cat possesses
      gall to glare at my poodle
sheltered by the taunt of glass.

But pink hyacinths—magnets
      to my eyes—jeweled crowns
rise as ecstatic congregants
      despite the crème & caramel cat
sullying dirt nearby. Still

emerald flat stalks—all with
      blooms supporting tiny,
peppermint goblets crowding close—
      a choir belting anthems.
They hold no cares
      for today & what's coming.

What Grass!

In remembrance of 2020, California fires

Grass taller than me. What power in pressing it down!
Grass for cloaking, we ardent teens secure our privacy.
Grass blows in April winds, transforms from lush to dry.
Grass shifting hues, sensuous green to sultry yellow.

Grass stiffening in hot force of July. Life fluid leaving.
Grass long dried summons a lightening surprise.
Grass fires spread. August threat to people, also beasts.

Fires Pillow Us

Our makeshift wire coop stands barren—
        no hen feathers or curious eyes
where I once tossed tofu to guests
rustling and thumping furious wings—
        twenty delicate heads hustled, bobbed,
and thrust—caramel & white feathered—
        riot for pale globs.

Gone that wild smoky time, where
        behind a pen marble eyes ogled me.
A return to azure skies—our air no longer
        stinks of smoldering fires.
Gone grandkids too—no more pranks—
        a boy's smelly socks
secreted within crannies of a couch.
Gone tender giggles or stumbles on red and yellow
        Lego structures for piracy or potions.

Goodbye to forty-minute crying jags
        from bodies tender and mercurial.
Goodbye to late-night chats with "kids" burgeoned to adults—
        heart-to-hearts while smaller ones slumber.
Goodbye to pasta and restricted diets. No more guardians
        coaxing stubborn mouths to open.
Goodbye to a favorite, bright magenta cup—
        necessary to hush a toddler's loud complaints.
Goodbye to hallway collisions—suitcase laundry
        requiring frequency washing. Still
honeyed hugs—leaning down or upright—linger
deep and cider memories pillow us—
        frosty hard and sweet.

Aftermath

The freshest of green
fern fronds flower forth
in fire's ashy ring.

Lime the Mud

At the International Wetland, Pt Reyes

Tourists gone, except us. We splurge for a sleep by water. Sun's up—mist makes all soft, hue of steel, uncertain, so like my trek of late. A white-tailed kite wings through, alone in frills of fog—no, a bird beneath flaps along at the very same rhythm. I'm wrong again—a water mirror made a twin, a presence that can't be touched. Can I fly in a curtain of mist—knowing I'm not alone?

While time sails on, fowl of brown poke beaks down, grasping mud snails from muck. Marbled Gobwit brunch too—year-round nesters. In life's last third the soiled and dank might feed me.

Where are the tens of thousands promised to winter here?

The mist draws back to tendrils—reveals an anchored trawler. One red line on its sullied white. Above, black wings beat, a string unfurling—sooty shearwaters go far. A single heron stands tall and regal, staring, still and ready to strike. Its spear yanks tiny sand dabs out. How many to fill its stomach? Tide ebbs—water recedes. Algae greens the mud stretching far and farther out.

California Hills, 4 P.M., Mid-April

I stoop here and there,
        opening my fists and heart
                to green, round hips of coastal hills,

proud as fecund mothers. They birth rapture with spritely
        masses of dots—pink, blue and violet flowers—
                come again despite a three-year drought.

While treading dirt trails, astonishments mount—
        long and slender leaves with ruffled edges vaunt
                cream blossoms—green frippery they seem.

No—the bulb beneath once gifted necessaries
        to the Miwok tribe: food, brushes, more—
                Soap Root it's named for cleansing.

Not far off, whimsy rules in raspberry puffs—nameless
        to untrained me—can their bitsy umbrella poofs
                shelter my mercurial mind? I who jig

to a mandolin, shifting, whirling from melancholy
        to awe or such meanness as fear imparts.
                Then come yearnings of a solitary sort.

Onward, Slender Cottonweed rises on long, scrawny
        stems and chides me. Their Q-tip ends lack vivacity
                of petals, yet simply charm.

If a genie granted choice, I'd be an oak, like this massive
        tree—green lost to winter, still majestic. Today
                emerald leafs out—a sturdy bulk, it lasts

and offers fingers of green with supple foliage quivering
desire. I thrill at woodsy summons, forego plans,
despite how bright beams fade and gusts
escort dusk's chill.

Island Serenity

Fallen for Serifos, Greece

Morning walk—finches chirp delicate
greetings. No rowdy crows of my Pacific
have flown this far. Geraniums redden
planters and oleander hedges trill their pink.
I eye the road, hug edge—so glad gardening
trucks of home don't rattle and roar.

A slim woman—in scarf-wrapped head and
loose black skirt brushing ankles—inspects
sparse shrubs and dirt afront her home and
bends straight from waist to yank out weeds—
      still limber at eighty. No return of
smile—we tourists come and go.

I breathlessly climb steep hills to pause,
revere what's beyond—white spreads, then blue
      bright blue of sea's dazzle, unlike
the gray to green of west-coast ocean.
By roadside, squat trees—olive and fig.
They bud green fruit within an arm's reach.

In town, billboard and neon cacophony absent.
Small stores with little signs—grocer, deli,
butcher, baker, swim boutique—enchant me.
      Few shoppers scurry. Waiters stroll
restaurant row—their leisurely way so soothing.
Linens, seaside and no need to call ahead.

California hustle shifts key and I tune myself
to mild slap of waters—shoulders soften.
      Oh, to take home within my suitcase
these melodies of sea and breeze.

Revolting Feet

We put one foot down,
        pick it up with little thought
for toes—digitorium to a doctor—attached
        to phalanx, metatarsals, and cuneiforms,
sizeable, palpable bones—
        little—unpondered—
yet they hold us upright,
        make feasible our reachings.

After the surgeon shaved the bunion off,
        for weeks these tiny, hard
              tissues screamed
      —hid beneath their tendons—
                sesamoids—they're called—
—yet who knows their names—even their
        existence—that we can't rise or walk
without their tender
        pulley action—we're ignorant
until the clamor and revolt.

Glimpsing the Better Part

Returned to my house, I wonder—what makes home?
In the tiny cabin I vacated, mislaid glasses reappeared—
not so within my many rooms. On needled paths I roamed—
here concrete pounds my feet, pine scent sadly absent.

Each comfort allures. In my garden, I spread my toes
in soft dirt—no need of sneakers' shelter. My vine
of green balls two weeks prior dangles soft red globes.
Inhale that heady scent—such multitudes all mine!

The plentiful life attracts but vexes. My serrated
knife—where can I find you? It slices tomato skin
and juicy orbs prove luscious. Ache for forest glens abates
but soon visions of the wild attract—a tossing within.

Ads besiege. They lure me to such frivolous spending
and bounty dwindles—oh, Spirit, keep me in true seeing.

Part IV

In my beginning is my end.
 —T. S. Eliot

Forgetting in Kauai

Fluted columns of Grecian imitation :: bear
lofty glory of courtyard roof :: no fencing off
      red spikes of ginger flowers :: long
and rounded leaves :: I don't deserve :: roof-high
sculptures :: gold-glossed murals :: pristine swans.

Plush pillows pad my back loafing on rattan ::
I lose myself :: float in womb of purest
aqua :: within a whale-sized ring :: pool's
      fountain marvel :: waterfall kneading
crimped shoulders :: crooning lulls me.

I muse :: what did local singers gross for
strums and songs :: created :: practiced after hours
      of wearing big smiles for island guests—
gentle when vexed :: Or the drudgery of office work.

Guests plane home :: few try tasty joints—local eats—
      and don't dare perch on benches' rutted seats ::
No seeing big shack city at nearby beach :: displaced
natives :: price of forced possession :: U.S presumptions.

A silver-haired scout :: skin of bronze :: yanks
weeds to keep resort lawn clean :: his wages
      a Waimea Canyon distant from :: techie ::
CEO or lawyer :: The calm Pacific surges :: Still

he answers my smile :: and with warm *Aloha* ::
      Such grace to put aside :: the history of
wrested rule of dirt and sea :: plantation cruelties ::
the lynchings :: white connivances to stop their protest.

On flying home :: will I forget? ::
    What can I :: remember—do? ::
    vote :: argue for :: a paying
back of what is due—

Strange Saint

Kateri lost all—
parents, sight, tribe to killing pox
blue-coat French brought—still

kept sky of inner sight
and fierce love of God. She took
food to her blue people.

Out of Alignment—Family Splits

α

Bavarian homes birthed Hitler
and Prince Rupert both—who
      proves ancestor to my German
name of Yaeger? I stand accused
of politics that betray my long-gone kin.

β

My mom played only with a ball as a child
in Oklahoma, knew only her mother, never father.
He'd ridden out to deliver mail in the time of
Spanish flu and news of him never returned.
The whole family bent to pluck cotton.
      Married, turned middle class, she yet
kept care for the laborer, the forgotten.
At thirty-some my parents-to-be moved West,
chose the Golden State—my place of birth,
school and play. Dad's family migrated too,
but Grandpa kept dancing his Ozark jigs
      for us four kids.

γ

I marry, turn mother. Years on, constraints
gone, I jet to Munich intent on my
      Bavarian heritage.
In Alpen foothills, windowsills boast rose geraniums,
      and pristine gardens—like that my parents tended.
In a Bavarian castle I read history—how Hitler approached
      Prince Rupert with an offer to restore Rupert
to kingship of this region. Rupert refused—

      Hitler couldn't play him for a fool.
The prince's homeland backed him, but Hitler's
      hoodlums forced his flight to Italy,
his princess into prison.

These days kin of mine embrace disinformation—
      succumb to deceit and condemn:
You shame our family name—
      out of alignment—
      I'm shunned.

From my eyes a saline shower
      floods my garden. I deadhead
a pink geranium—Mom's favorite—my own
      shrub grew big from her cutting—
her blooms open in me.

Bald Eagle

Webs spun over the hard and calculating
    eye of a black, iron-hard
        yard ornament.

White strings spun by countless eight-
    legged creatures—each line slim and
        flimsy—yet together

weave a robust net over the regal bird's gaze
    where a gargantuan, malevolent
        spider seizes shelter.

The breeze coming off the Hood Canal does not
    rattle the sticky clasp. No recapture of
        the eagle's vision—

democracy entrapped. Numerous threads concoct
    this web so tight: media fabrications, power plays,
        and pig-headed, partisan ploys. Gone fair sight.

American Eagle rendered blind.

Misguided Spring

January first our fence's jasmine
        vine lays bare—no scent.
On inauguration day, looking dirt-wise,
green and pointed tips push up
        through my garden's loose soil—
they whisper as a kettle nearing boil—above a wan
        sky. That news broadcast—a well-crafted
speech pledged much. Out back a shiny crow
        caws and gathers a murder.

In February's start, soft swords in the yard
daily grow longer—gentle fronds.
        Quince flowers murmur sweet—
beware
        its thorns. Mid-month daffodils, burst out—

sunshine encased buds or unbolted to heated
        yellow—like a Hawaiian sun—
pointed edges of these crowns
promise much—winsome governance?

Yet while songbirds warble, this morning
the ice of their bath lies thick.
        Still. Silent. Shaggy fleece
snuggles my arms—I open my eyes—
        squeezed and news weary
              —find my apricot tree buds

vulnerable as pale nipples. Warning—
        a chill blast of wind—will it drop
the fruit? I dare not hide my jacket over a hook
        or maintain naïve belief
              in the swell of
any politician.

Find a Drop of Blood

The deputy in slacks and knee-high boots heaves
a weighty door—neglect, injury, violence.
They've come to lead a prayer service, she tells forty
        females wearing thin orange uniforms.

They scatter round a large, cool room—walls empty
of all color. A resident, standing in her four-bed section,
spies over the divider to the next. Cameras point
        all places—even within the toilet stalls.

Eight shamble out—tall and squat, obese and trim.
        They dismantle stacks of seats. We form
a circle on well-scuffed vinyl to read aloud, pray, and hear
their worries—mothers, kids, addiction, and the system.

A voice quivers—like a ball atop a net—
        a slight woman with a blonde bob. Her hands
envelop her small ears: *The voices—I can't stop them,*
        can't get my schizophrenia meds.

When the group departs, another speaks—a model
beauty with clear dark skin, hair curled close.
She leans to me and whispers—*The spirits command me:*
        find a murdered one—leave a drop of blood.
Matthew's spirit keeps speaking. Can't you hear him?

Sorry, no. Must be scary. I do what I know—
        pray by name, copy digits from her band
to bring help later. A name matters little here.
Still she insists I write hers down—*Don't forget me.*
        Her full moon, frightened eyes sear me.

Deputies with handguns and ponytails dismiss us
        with no thought. Our path crosses cracked
asphalt by sharp, ashen buildings, soaring fences—
        with massive metallic spirals, ferocious spikes atop.

My partner punches a secret code. The last gate swings open.
        Home by freeway to rooms with knobs that turn,
precious privacy and medicine for my taking.
        For many nights and days, this beauty and
her tragedy remain close with me.

Monticello Marvels

α

I walk the mount to the ever-famed Monticello mansion.
Pristine trim, octagonal dome awe—Jeffersonian style,
what Thomas combined of Neoclassical & Roman styles
he'd admired overseas—one of few super-rich travelers then.

Triple paned windows & curved bricks—innovative.
Curtains colored mustard & golden walls—adapted
from French fashions—forged by kidnapped peoples
you, Thomas, called your own. Your soft gentleman's

hands—never clutch the whip, build again—
You build & build—grow your debt—necessitate
others' grueling servitude. Scarce food. No end. You pen
slavery wrong but carry on with "negro family"—illusion.

After the death of your wife Martha, you suffer grief.
You voyage to Paris & call your daughters & enslaved
Sally to travel also. Do you own the strangeness—
young Sally as half-sister to your vanished Martha?

β

Sally, your alacrity & grace blazed when you spun wool
into thread in a hovel—standing out among the many dark
offspring. Now no choice but to sail and leave all dear.
You wash and mend as the ship's deck pitches.

You gape at Parisian grand monuments at fourteen.
Never allowed choices, living on the brink, you can't say
No, to the avid hands of Master Thomas. Yet you keep
more in mind—over time you sway him. He grants you

exceptional concessions. We call it strange that you left
French freedom, but you're pregnant—what for you, solitaire,
in Paris? Back home, you gain a room of your own. More—
Thomas promises to liberate your children. At his death.
He orders you served his delights—trout, pasta, & more—
unlike your previous pittance.

You weep when you lose his baby, but the night-time
trysts don't end. In your time you cradle his
seed in your cave-like room under parquet floors.
And more babies through the years.

Your little children hammer, dig, spin, & wait on table—
dawn to dark with fifty others. Your hands deform—
your veins protrude—from carrying trays, shining silver,
scrubbing dishes. At nightfall, finally allowed to still.

Still, you're wanted—you press & soothe his tight thighs,
stroke his sandy hair & pale chest. You never fail
to gaze into his eyes. You know his need of love.
Do you name it so in your quarters? You've become

an expert at persuasion of your virtue—
you use him for your purpose.

A Large Room's Sole :: Light

Step onto the white plastered pavement. See one big, old house :: You ponder :: much paint missing :: multiple white dots flecked off of dull moss color :: It all signs little care :: start of the wrong.

Two doors in front :: Choose your steps because no clear walk can be seen :: around the side more doors and locks :: Twenty-five folks within? :: No one knows the residents.

A Denver investor bought this apartment :: in a town stinking of meat and sugar beet processing :: You bet he never made the hour-drive here :: never seen the insides as you view today :: at least this landlord :: doesn't freeze his tenants out :: or raise the rent.

Four units of asylum seekers :: refugees from tribal wars :: survive in this decrepit house sectioned off :: no AC :: uneven heat :: space heaters needed. Tenants labor in varying shifts :: night or day :: can't gather to portion their bills from a sole meter.

Disrepair beyond what you can fathom :: large, dark rooms where all light comes from a single, dim ceiling bulb :: half-only curtains :: ragged sheets on windows :: no seats, bath or kitchen fan.

A black man on the floor faces a mammoth TV :: Does he long for his home's vast grasslands pictured on the giant screen?

A gargantuan tarantula of mold sprawls on a window :: fearing to breathe, you rush on. Nearby, a kitchen floor buckles :: rising like a wave :: you leap off :: scared you'll sink :: Paint peeling from sheetrock nears size of a bedsheet.

What do you expect from a 93% white town? Some say: *I don't want Somalians on my block ::* Rental properties known :: by word of mouth :: refugees offered only debris.

Solemn, dark faces hint at loss :: anguish beyond knowing. Is it running from a machete's slice? A child shot :: bleeding out :: What grim scenes haunt?

Because you heard of recommended potential :: to better this place you flew here :: Seeing all, you feel a punch in the gut :: recoil.

In another unit :: a toddler throws himself down :: on seeing pale-faced you :: His mother takes him up :: Her ruby smile gleams.

Bright yellow, emerald and sapphire cloth :: of glorious African motif :: winds around her survivor's heart :: Strong arms bind her boy to her bosom :: and her brave core brimming with love.

After Morning News

After I heard the election results //
       only a primary // but still telling

so very much // I wanted to raise a fist
       flailing the air // flashing like Zeus my rage //

or to froth a riverbed //
       with white-tongued // capsizing currents //

yet I didn't // went on pacing to a hum-drum job //
       while aching, wanting this time // this nation

to be a listening place // not where power wielders grab
       from farm laborers // or factory workers // that pale-

skinned dozers like me // would jerk awake and do something
       to stop professionals thieving // systemic // bigotry //
and police violence //

a way // that millionaires // who back an issue // or a candidate //
       did not steer // what and who wins // that the plethora

of shiny bright-hued mailers—what realtors or other
       power brokers fund // accomplish nil //

that ordinary // human basic
       needs // could triumph.

Nectared Quiet

Nearby a whirr so fast
we can't see wings. Oh, to have
      his dexterity! His delicacy.
The hummer lingers quite near—my right side,
      left side, then my back till he's convinced
my gardenia scent can't be sipped.
      Nothing here for him.
Chin up—petulant, he protests—parades
      his crimson flag and leaves me.
Our talk returns to rising prices and politics.

Days later, a sprawling, wintery bush has turned
      extravagant with a blooming parade.
We sit near it, so the hummer perches on a clothesline
      and glares—*won't you leave? At least hush?*

We quiet. He's mere brown—like a wren—
      but amazing speed and
           miniature form enchants us.

He stares & shifts his teensy-weensy bead
      of an eye, vexed at intruders who sit
in his domain. He dares closer
      to a small white blossom.
Past the outer, tiny fan of coral,
      he inserts a spear-like beak.
Turned careless of our easy reach, he hums
      and sips from another.

Our lips stay sealed, our drinks unlifted,
      our arms stilled—
such thrill at passing his strange test.
      Awe. Silence. Such
nectared solace—nothing else sounds but
      a bee's faint buzzing.

To Nike of Athens

Nike means victory

Oh, you of dusty hillsides, stony
terraces, fig trees, ice white stucco
cities—your venerators birthed citizen's vote.

Your freemen in tunics argued
rules, the need to placate weary
slaves. Give them plays! Distract.

Oh Goddess, of gorgeous, marble Temple,
in luscious drapes of stone linen, you've lost
your head. Your sight vanished. You can't see

chained immigrants. You stand on measured
boulders trimmed, aligned to rocks, making pavement
within stone cut walls that mesmerize—what Greek feats.

Will you question their myths? Their kind
of democracy not bestowed on all. You, Goddess,
won't you fight for people of all hues, all stations?

Oh Nike, hear the sage owl's hoot!

Do you know Ares rampages and propagates
hellish lies? See the throes of those
his nail sharp boot tramples underfoot.

I'll be your eyes, oh Goddess! Can I tell
you how noble dreams die when rule and power
are not fairly shared with others. Oh, Nike,

rebirth yourself! You bare strong, marble shoulder
and stoop for sandal—now strap it tight! Take up
impervious helmet and stretch out your brilliant wings.

Wasting Time in Greece

After Elizabeth Bishop's ironic travel poems

Frivolous arches & precision-cut stone
form their walls by road, sugar
cube houses—enchant me
at first, but from constant heat
no relief. What will I do?

I try the beach. Coarse sand
grates feet. Near naked bodies,
so browned, so taut—my stomach roll
should not be seen. What's to do
for a senior?

Aegean diamonds dazzled
the day before & before that. Never
do lullabies roll. At home, Pacific
mists cool, but what's to do
here—shop for dark glasses?

Why doesn't this café stock
decaf? Forget eggplant mush.
No more tomatoes—perhaps
garlic snails can catalyze
contentment. But now

what's for me?
Facebook posts!
"Take my photo!" I snap
& the scruffy faced waiter
does as I ask.

His pic captures my grin and
sunscreened cheeks. Perhaps
my posted digital hearts
will capsize my small-town
blues. May wind over this Aegean
sea plumb my depths and rescue me.

Colors Blend

Gyroscope swirls—bold
sky, stars whirl, garden
mingle—unity.

Bursting Out

Milkwood munching caterpillar turned to pupa bursting out—
        orange and brown. Black outlines. Monarch
                flutters from my eager eyes.
Mary, you knew transformations—babe suckling on milk-ripe
        breasts vanished at thirteen. Fear squeezed.
Reclaiming him at the temple, you protest—no Madonna
        smile for errant child. Yet he claims his rightness.

When you confront him at thirty at the bridal party—
        "Woman, what have I to do with you?" His words
                gravel down your tender palate. Yet he does
what you ask—household water into vats of heady drink.

His brothers clamor through the crowd years later. "Come on
        home!" It's your dread that sent his brothers to command
                him stay his death mission. "Doing what God
wants is what births a person as my kin!" What chiding.
        Does heat flush your slender neck and cheeks?
                He forges ahead, accepting of his torture

at Golgatha's crest. You bow your head, hear him heaving
        for his breath. Does his splay of limbs on splintered
                timbers pierce your own? Do you wrestle with
a horrid creature? What roils your heart's deep sea?

Three days after, he offers palms with blood-rimmed holes.
        Do you lean damp cheeks on his chest? Unfathomable
thrumming of his lavish heart. Do you wonder at the broken
        chrysalis? Tremble when his eerie yet same body departs?
Your baby, toddler, teen, and man gone.

Solace of touch no more. Without him, bereft and torn
        till John finds you, gives a solid, sweat-tinged hug—
Do paper-thin wings beat around you—thrill of orange
        outlined with black. Can you hear the
pulse of spring in winter's dearth and eerie calm?

Spiraling Songs

At 4 a.m. on my bed I succumb.
That old and guttural Hiss—
the Demon of Self-Accusation—
pulls on me. I fall deep
in a desolate mine shaft
where midnight waters seep.

But I come to listen to the spacious
Voice, the ever-present, ever-loving
Wisdom (not that *prove yourself, fit in
with others, must get-it-right* obsession).
I turn, attend and my subterranean
Soul perceives true Love.

The Spirit throws a rope ladder.
My fingers clasp its coarse fibers
to climb up and out. Embraced—
joy in who I am, accepted
with what I'm not.

She points me to a staircase
for winding up immensity of
her giant Tree, past gnarls, lines,
and furrows. I ascend past nests
birthing finch, crow, and sparrow alike.
They open beaks miniscule and long,
blunt and keen. I graze myself
on sharp points, but aloe
leaves bring balm. Songs of joy
and tenderness float around
the Tree of Life—I spiral up.

Notes

"A Large Room's :: Sole Light" derives from observing firsthand and learning second-hand from some compassionate Americans (such as IAFR) who work with those forcibly displaced. The African refugees typically work in sugar beet and meat packing processing and scanty housing is available for them.

All poetry is partially or totally fiction. Please know I hold my siblings in love and compassion and think of them often. Maturing for me has involved realizing that boundaries are good and that sometimes, despite our deepest desire to do so, we cannot drop our baggage.

About the Author

Carol L. Park grew up halfway between San Jose and San Francisco, leaving and returning many times, but remaining a California girl—until she spent six years immersed in Japan, having moved to Tokyo with her husband and two children. Her style of communication and relationships have evolved from that experience and 35 years of marriage to a magnificent Korean-American computer engineer. Decades back, she shocked and annoyed her mother by requiring her to follow a new household custom: to take off shoes before entering. Carol credits her and her dad, both raised in Oklahoma, for her radical hospitality, gardening, and determination. As a child, before it was popular to disdain the old Barbie, she did, throwing away mascara to climb peaks and gaze in wonder at waterfalls and redwoods. From early on, reading and writing stories and poems delighted her, but she didn't develop the craft until later in life.

TESOL (Teaching English to Speakers of Other Languages) has brought Carol into a myriad of new recipes and fresh views. Among her travel joys have been America's southwest and east coast, Vietnam, Taiwan, Spain, Italy, France, and Durango, Mexico. Her six years in Tokyo and Kobe proved the best and hardest part of her life. One more transforming experience: volunteering in a jail. Carol has learned to adapt to a yet-different culture and seen the outcome of our unjust system.

The best compliment of Carol's twenties was, *You don't judge.* Of her thirties: *You're a good mother.* Of her forties: *You're very generous.* Fifties: *You bring people together.* Of her sixties: *You've re-made yourself into a writer.*

Find more of Carol's words at
www.carolpark.us

www.ingramcontent.com/pod-product-compliance
Lightning Source LLC
Chambersburg PA
CBHW030051170426
43197CB00010B/1479